I'd like to dedicate this book to all those I've loved and lost by death, especially my husband, Stephen, and my grandson, Gordon.
I love you with an everlasting love.

Introduction

Effective communication takes a variety of skills to master in the best of situations. Our need for contact and connection with others is paramount to our survival in all cultures. Sharing ideas and feelings and developing relationships helps us to make meaning out of our existence. In the process of communication, we develop community. Sometimes, certain situations get in the way of effective communication.

When we are overcome with grief, it's as though a mental roadblock has been erected, surrounding us in vague exits and entrances. At times, it seems as though we've forgotten what's appropriate, how to respond to others, or even how to find peace and serenity within. After a death takes place, confusion and emotions take over rationality as we continue to adapt, adjust and interpret our new reality. Making meaning out of our grief causes an internal struggle with the self, too. Giving meaning to the experience of grief becomes necessary if we are to continue our connection with others.

I have found that grief is pointless unless we give voice to the pain that begins at the top of our heads and descends to the tips of our toes. We must allow ourselves to communicate in any way we can to release the multitude of feelings we try so hard to bury. Our "selves" deserve to be heard, expressed and comforted as we validate the memories of those who are gone. We need to speak, write, dance, draw or act out the message of grief so that we may find our own healing moments. Then, we can identify again with the world around us with more meaning and with needed connections. This is how the barrier of grief can be penetrated as we gain new skills of confidence, insight and strength to once more make meaning out of our lives.

Healing Moments

I

LOOSE CHANGE

During grieving periods in my life, I've heard a lot of stories from others about "Pennies from heaven." I've had many loved ones who died, and I believed that when I saw a penny on the ground, it was a special sign from them. They were there with me, unseen. Those pennies tended to bring me so much comfort, especially when I needed it most.

My late husband and I used to pick up loose change we found on our daily walks. It became a game for us as we tallied up the amount we had collected and tossed into a small jar. Once, at the end of the year, we had collected over twenty-five dollars. After he died, I picked up change to continue the game, but mostly because it made me feel that somehow he was with me, close by again. I felt comforted by that old belief that the pennies were a sign, but I was never able to collect anywhere near what we had collected together.

He's been gone for a few years now, and I've adjusted to a different life without him. I still miss him and wish he were with me on those lonely walks, picking up loose change. Lately, I've just been leaving the change on the ground. Maybe, I don't believe in the "Pennies from heaven" story anymore, or maybe I've moved beyond the intense need to know he's still there in my life. Today, I can leave the change for others to pick up so they might feel their loved ones are close to them. Knowing that others can work through their grief issues and feel comforted by the loose change they find, gives me comfort, if only for the moment.

Healing Moments

2

SIGNS OF GRIEF

I always know when the widow down the street is going through a grieving period. She comes home in the late evening, turns the lights down low and puts on various styles of music. Sometimes, it's old melodies from her youth, classical renditions, or spiritual chants such as vespers. She turns the music up loud so that it fills the air and drifts down the street. Sometimes it catches me off guard and brings me to tears of compassion for what she must be suffering.

Since I'm not her, I can't imagine what she feels, but I do empathize with her as I see images moving around the room. I can imagine her wandering from room to room, searching for the ghosts of the past until she settles into a chair where probably she and her husband used to cuddle in the evening. Alone, she reminisces about past events and how she misses the most important connection she ever had. Sadly, she dances alone until she tires of the melodies and stops the music, turns off the light and retreats to the bed she and her husband shared. Repeatedly, she once again says her nightly ritual of prayers and waits for the morning. Lying there alone, she tosses and turns, restless, until she grabs a pillow to hold onto as if it could fill the void in her soul. Sometimes, she gets up and wanders through the moonlit rooms, possibly getting something to eat to ease her anxiety. Or she may take another bath before she finally settles in comfortably. At last, she falls asleep, sheathed in the darkness of the night.

When I see her the next day, she seems more spirited and happy. I assume she's worked through yet another stage of her personal pain. I'm happy for her as we walk along talking about her plans for the day, knowing that she may again need to pull the curtains tight as she processes her loss, but for now she's out and about living life actively.

Healing Moments

3

NEW VISTAS

Sundays were always special days for my husband and me. After breakfast and church, we would map out plans for the ride we would take into the countryside, traveling down roads that would take us into wooded areas, lake fronts, ravines and occasional hilltops with panoramic views. After he died, I tried a few times on my own to repeat the scenarios, but it never felt quite the same alone. Realizing that special someone to talk with, explore with or to just sit with on those drives was missing, I decided to just take a break for awhile. I found other things to do on Sundays. I also knew I was a bit frightened of getting lost or maybe having a flat tire and being alone on a deserted back road. For a long time, I felt helpless and unsure of myself.

Recently, I had the urge to go for a long, wandering ride as we had done in the past. As I drove down old familiar territory, I decided to try a new route to see where I would end up. "Pretty brave, but where am I going?" I said to myself. Gaining confidence, I followed a road as it twisted in and out, up and down, along paths that hadn't been used in a long time. As I continued, I decided to take a turn that would present something totally surprising to me. The road brought me to a beautiful vista where a vast stretch of blue water appeared on the horizon. As I admired the beautiful scenery and got my boundaries firmly in place, I cried with delight. I recognized where I was and slowly meandered down the road into familiar territory again. Now, I felt confident that I could navigate successfully and arrive home safely. Those roads reminded me of the twists and turns that grief takes us on emotionally as we work through feelings, endings, beginnings and new comfort zones. Grief has its own paths. Sometimes the paths are clear for us, but at other times, we question the way to go. We'll find the way as time heals and gives us new vistas. We'll look back knowing we made it home successfully. We'll find the way home and be grateful for the ride we took and the confidence we gained.

Healing Moments

4

RUNNING ON EMPTY

While I was driving to the grocery store for my weekly supply of food and other essentials, I looked at the gas gauge. The needle was pointing to the large E that registered as empty. "I need to get gas," I said, "but when?" I had too much to do and I had felt completely overwhelmed since the death of my husband. Yet another demand on my time and energy was annoying. As I turned the corner, I saw a large blue sign that announced a full-service gasoline station, so I pulled in. Just as I was about to get out of the car, a young man came over and asked if I'd like help filling my tank. Surprised at the offer, I relaxed and said, "Oh, sure, that would be fine!" As I watched him wash my windshield, I realized how I, too, had been running on empty. Grief had drained my energy as I kept myself busy enough to not want to think or feel anything. Running from the pain seemed the easier route, but I still felt the emptiness of the lost connections with family and friends. My emotional tank was empty, and I needed to surrender to the efforts that would fill me up as well as give me the energy to move forward on my grief path.

Some things I needed to do were obvious. First, I needed to slow down and stop running away. I needed to rethink priorities in my new life. I had to ask myself some serious questions that day: "How important is it that some things just don't get done? How can I help restore myself? What do I really need right now?" It felt as if I sat there for a long time before the young man finished his work, but it felt good to be waited on. As I paid him, I thanked him with a big smile and turned the car around. Realizing that I was tired, I went home to take a long nap in the middle of the day. That refreshing rest gave me a more restored attitude; grief is work and I had already put in a full day. A break was in order before I broke! That gas gauge had become my personal checkpoint of how I'm doing emotionally and physically. It may seem silly, but now I check it every day.

Healing Moments

5

RAINBOWS

As I rested there on the floor, I gazed up at the ceiling and saw a strange reflection from the window. The image appeared to be a paintbrush and just below it were two rainbows. I looked around the room to see where the color was coming from, but I couldn't find anything. Still mesmerized by the image, I thought about the Master Artist and the Universal Rainbow that often appears after a rainstorm. I also thought about how refreshing and joyful one feels at the sight of that arched image. It reminded me of the storm of grief after my husband died that seemed to make a lake of tears before I could stop crying. Rainbows didn't appear to me at that time because I couldn't see anything clearly. I couldn't see a future without my husband; I couldn't see how God had plans for me. And I certainly couldn't see the gift of new life at the end of the rainbow.

As the months and years slowly advanced, the sun began to shine through the huge cloud of my tears. My life began to fill up with new activities that provided the sense of direction I had not had during that intense early grieving period. Eventually, the curtain of grief was drawn back to reveal brighter days, enhanced relationships, hope for new beginnings and the sense of purpose I needed to go forth in a wonderful world. The image of the two rainbows made me realize that I had had a colorful life with my husband, but I also had another colorful life ahead of me. The Master Artist is still at work painting rainbows after the clouds pass away. Maybe it's just the angle we approach things from that makes the difference; maybe it's all in the timing. Or, maybe it's when our hearts are open to new beginnings that brighter days lay ahead of us. There is hope at the end of the rainbow. There is new life! There is new joy! That's the pot of gold!

Healing Moments

6

TREADMILLS

Manage my own life?! I'm getting tired of all the yard work, and I'm not even too con-cerned about it lately. I seem to have less energy for some things. I guess it's because I got off the treadmill. After my husband died, I worked hard to keep his gardens in full bloom as I had promised when he was sick and we were discussing options for the yard in the future. I felt on top of everything with an I-can-do-it attitude, so I decided to be brave, follow through on his wishes and make others feel good by showing that I'm adjusting. That treadmill must have been going full speed and I didn't even realize it. I guess it was the pain in my arm that finally cued me to lower the throttle to at least half speed. I certainly didn't want to break down.

My grief needed to be tended to also, so I hired others to do what I was not able to accomplish by myself. Besides, I really didn't have to do everything alone. Maybe it was my way of being closer to my husband as I tended to his lovely gardens and realized how much he must have cared for them. I learned to develop an "easy-does-it" style and let go of managing the outcome of grief's landscape. Nature took its course in spring, summer, fall and winter, because each season has its own areas of warmth and cold.

I can't get around to all the work left behind that two might accomplish together, but I'm living outside the garden walls now, meeting and managing life at a slower pace. And, I might add, enjoying the pleasures of each day while I watch the breaking forth of new life. Now, the garden has a few more weeds each year and there are more cracks in the sidewalk, but I know I'll get around to fixing them someday. Someday I'll get around to it, but not today.

Healing Moments

7

THE SORROW THAT STILL COMES

I didn't want to have to sell the car we had come to love so much as part of our "new life" since the children had grown up. The car had made us feel young again as we sped down the highway, weaving in and out in traffic. But my husband had told me I should let it go or it would cost me too much to keep it up. Even when he was dying, he worried about how I would manage finances and house repairs, let alone a sports car that was what he considered "high-maintenance." A year after he died, I struggled as I tried to hold on and let go at the same time, which really doesn't work. Little by little, I found that I could let go of those things that we had shared as a couple. Sure, there were tears and some remorse, but very little regret since I took my time and allowed the grieving process to work its healing magic. However, every time I saw a similar car on the highway, it brought back thoughts of the good old days.

I still have wonderful memories of the fun times, but if I still had the car, I might still have the pain. Yes, the sorrow continues when I have to part with a treasure from the love of my life, but I allow myself the time and tears it takes to work through whatever it is I need in order to get to the other side of grief. That other side is where acceptance and the desire to live and watch the blooming of my new life takes place. I've been separated from those I've loved and still love, and I would like the sorrow to stop forever, but I know that is part of the human connection. Today, my ability to feel is a gift for me, and it came because I loved someone deeply. My sorrow is mixed with the fondest of memories. My sorrow reminds me of my connections to others.

Healing Moments

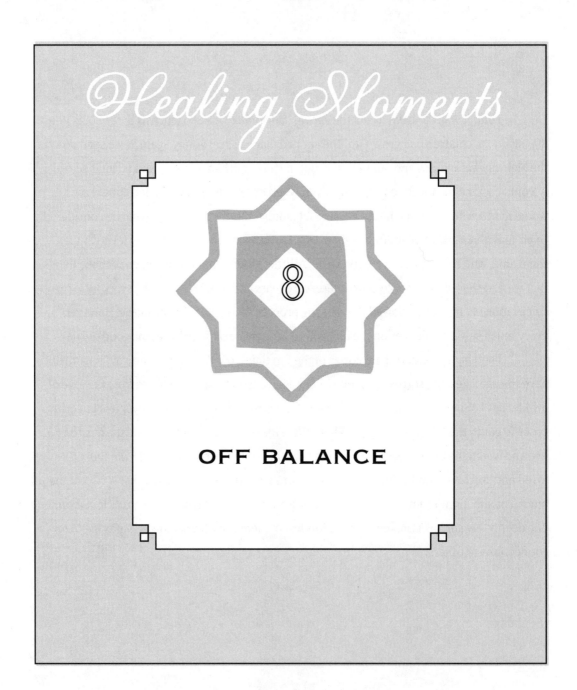

8

OFF BALANCE

Every spring and fall I change the curtains and bedding accessories. A new look always makes me feel refreshed, and it gives me a signal to change inwardly, too. I had a wonderful, sunny day to work and began diligently to create a new look. I began taking the curtains down and dusting a bit. As I put up the new curtains, it was a struggle to balance the rod. Doing this alone has always been a problem for me. Slowly, I worked the fabric toward the other end and just as I put up the finishing touch, the whole rod collapsed on the floor. Frustrated, I picked it up again as the twisted mess began to wobble back and forth. As I wrestled with balancing the rod, I began to intermittently cry and sigh with grief. I felt so alone in my simple task and wished I had my husband there to share the load and help me.

Finally, with rod intact, I was finished, but as I climbed off the stool to admire my work, I realized the curtains were not even. One side was at least a foot longer than the other side. I had been able to balance the center perfectly, but there was unevenness in the overall picture. That's how I'd been feeling since my husband died a couple of years ago. Grief issues cause my balance to be off at times, and I feel crooked—just like those curtains. That's the way it is for now. I believe if I can understand it and then accept it, maybe I'll heal a little bit more. I can't change the affect that death has had on me until I change my need for balance. Today, I'm accepting "off-balance" as a more real way to view life. It certainly is less stressful. I never did balance those curtains that day. When I woke up the next morning, I just chuckled. It was a small thing to worry about. True balance had come in the way I saw things after that experience. Maybe, I could start a new trend by being "off balance."

Healing Moments

9

NOT TODAY

When the gentleman walked into the office, he was in a hurry. I thought maybe he was late for a meeting. We glanced at each other and then went about our business. I finished my work a few minutes later and brought it to an assistant. As I looked up, the man was wandering in the hall as if searching for something. Finally, when someone from another office spoke to him, I heard him say, "I'm looking for the widow/widowers meeting."

He was directed to a room down the hall, but I had already seen him glance into that room and walk away. Then I heard him say, "Not today, I guess" and I watched a change come over him as he hurriedly exited the building. That brought me back to an earlier time when I had come to the same meeting. My husband had just died, and I just didn't want to face anyone.

"Not today, when I have to face my world alone. Not today, when others remind me that someone they've cared about has also died suddenly—or slowly. Not today, because I hurt too much and don't want others to see it. Not today, because my grief is too new. Not today, because I see your pain and it's just too hard to look in the mirror. There's still time to face the loneliness, rebuild my life, and get the courage to go on with only memories to cherish. People are ready when they're ready, not a minute sooner or later, and I'm not ready today. Not today; just not today."

It takes a lot of courage to walk into a support group the first couple of times. The awkwardness of feeling so naked and raw in the grip of grief can send us running out the door before we even begin to shed the skin of the past and renew ourselves in vulnerable moments with others. Maybe not today, we think, but when?

I'm glad I finally walked through the doors to face the grief that can cripple us at times. I'm glad I allowed myself to be vulnerable in the face of others. And I'm glad to be involved with a group of individuals who have courage, strength and hope to deal with the issues that surface during the intense grieving period. As we bond together, we find ourselves knowing what we can do today and not wait for tomorrow. We can do today! We can!

10

FAIRY TALES

I was babysitting for my fifteen-month-old grandson the other day, and as I read some books to him, I came across a collection of old fairy tales I had learned as a child. I thought about how significant fairy tales are to us as early teachers in how to perceive the world around us. "Little Bo-Peep has lost her sheep and doesn't know where to find them." "Mary had a Little Lamb," "Jack be Nimble; Jack be Quick," and "Who's Afraid of the Big Bad Wolf" are just a few of the nursery rhymes we learned as children that can impact us today at unconscious levels. Those rhymes serve to guide us in how to relate to the world around us when things get confusing, and things do get confusing when we grieve.

For months after my husband died, I felt like the "Big Bad Wolf" was at the door and all the locks, garlic and strength I had couldn't keep him at bay. Those wolves came in an array of sizes, colors and moods. The paperwork, chores and busyness of the day were just a few of the wolves. Others were those who were trying to sell me insurance, condos, stocks, bonds, etc. At times, I just wanted to lock the doors and stay alone, fearful that if I went outside another wolf would be around the corner. I thought I would never get through what I had to accomplish or keep the wolves from knocking on my door, but I did.

By tackling just one thing at a time, I was able to regain a sense of control, new confidence and my trust in humanity again. When the old friends stopped calling, I made new ones. I found new work to inspire personal growth, and I became an advocate for tenderhearted people who needed the same faith, hope and courage to live after the death of a loved one. All those fairy tales I remembered reading had good endings in spite of the tragedies that befell some of the characters. It may be a childhood fantasy, but I'm an adult now and I plan on having a good ending, too. And, when the wolves are at the door, whether real or imagined, I'll just "huff and puff" right back.

Healing Moments

II

FROZEN

The first time I went to a bereavement group, I watched the other individuals talk about the deaths of their own mates with such seeming ease. I wondered how could they be so relaxed and intimate with strangers. I certainly couldn't express my innermost feelings at a time when I was in such intense shock. As I continued to listen, the coordinator of the group turned to me and began asking questions. I felt frozen as her words rang in my ears. I could only nod or shrug my shoulders. While others seemed to easily discuss their personal experiences, I never said a word or shed a tear that night. My frozen state of being was a way for me to shut down all that I was feeling inside for fear that I would burst before the people in the room and embarrass myself. My pain was carefully hidden behind my cool aloofness, but I knew it was there. Like icicles hanging from a rooftop during a cold winter season, I wasn't ready to thaw just yet.

During a coffee break, I decided to leave and as I was walking out the door, someone shouted, "Come back again." I felt seen but not threatened. I just wasn't ready to share my pain with others. Every week when I returned to the group, I would leave during the coffee break. Safely outside, I could release some of the strongest emotions I would ever experience. "This grief thing is impossible," I told myself, but I kept coming back. Then during one session, I couldn't stop the tears from flowing down my cheeks. Others began to stare at me, but I didn't care as my face reddened with the burn of anger, sadness, fear and confusion. After the torrent of tears, I sensed a new feeling of peace. I realized there was hope that I could make it through this frosty crust I was creating by not allowing myself to accept my grieving nature. I think I actually began to smile more and relax a bit as I allowed others to warm and support me. I began to melt. I felt so good as we all discussed how death had affected us. That day, I knew if I kept coming back, my frozen self would turn into a warm, tender heart of compassion, and I would be able to share the benefits I have achieved through facing my grief.

Healing Moments

12

REFLECTIONS

Summer was ending, and as I was completing my morning journal reflections, I heard the sound of a flock of geese who were obviously heading south to a warmer climate. It reminded me of how many times I'd heard that sound and the odd feelings it stirred within me. That sound signals that we're headed for winter with closed doors and windows and shorter, darker days. My husband had died in the middle of the summer when the warmth of the sun surrounded me. The approach of winter made me wonder how I would make it through the cold months alone and the calamities that might happen. The elements I had to face alone aroused all my insecurities. As summer turned into fall, and then into winter, I cocooned my grief. The darkness of night made it easy for me to hide so others couldn't see my sorrow. The cold weather and snowy periods kept me inside while I healed from the wounds grief had inflicted on me.

Gradually, as winter turned into spring, the days again became longer and the nights shorter, and one morning I again heard the sound of geese flying overhead as their homecoming signaled the return of warmer weather. It made me think about how I had managed my first winter. What had seemed to be a dark tunnel of grief had opened out into brighter days. I was so grateful for the turning point that had helped me to accept nature's way of teaching and guiding me through the seasons of life. There are beginnings, middles and endings. There are periods of darkness and light. And there are times where we are dormant but growth is still taking place. Grief is like the cold hard winters in the Northern Hemisphere. It's a rough time, and getting through it is challenging, but hope emerges as we allow nature to take its course— just like the call of the geese changing direction for their survival.

Healing Moments

I3

SMALL TALK

We stood along the wall of the theater, exchanging small talk as we waited for the director to open the door. About a year after my husband died, I started ushering. I needed to fill the lonely nights with something interesting where I could meet new people who had similar interests. I had spent the first year after his death in a whirlwind of activities with friends, but as time went on, our lives adjusted and the connections decreased. I felt ready to try something different and wanted to begin to integrate into my new world as a widow. Taking a chance to meet new people and help myself was the best thing I could have done. As my interests in outside activities increased, I gradually began to feel more alive. On the nights I ushered, there was always somebody I knew from work or other environments. Socializing was therapeutic for me as I adjusted to my new life.

Many of the other ushers I met were also widows, and I began to accept this passage into a new normal. When Faith began talking to me, she eased into the conversation about her past life and the business she had shared with her husband before he left her. I thought that maybe this man had been going through a "mid-life" crisis, especially when she said, "for good." I was wondering how many times he had left when I realized she meant he had died. In the next few moments, we bonded in a special way with similar circumstances and time lines. It had been three years for both of us, and we were beginning to feel like our old selves again. We were smiling more, risking more and settling down more to a new type of "single" existence. Sure, our families were still there for us, but in a different way. We both still struggled with rebuilding our lives and wondered about how our futures would unfold. But, does anybody really know how their future will unfold? Maybe, we'll get to usher again someday or maybe I'll call her and we'll go to lunch. Either way, we connected in some small way by sharing those special moments.

Healing Moments

14

I WISH YOU WERE HERE

As I walked past the colorful shop windows, sun shining brightly, I thought about times past when my husband would beckon me closer to look at the merchandise displayed in the shop windows. Suddenly, an odd feeling arose within me and I couldn't stop the tears or memories from rushing forward. When my husband died, I lost a special window-shopping and strolling companion. My eyes wandered toward other couples who were holding hands, giggling and tugging at each other. As I walked alone, I remembered my familiar times when we were a couple.

Tears trickled down my cheeks and I could almost hear the silent words, "I wish you were here with me to enjoy the day. I wish you were holding my hand and giggling with me. I wish you were here to help guide me along unfamiliar streets. I just wish you were here!" As the emotion and words collided, I felt grief momentarily ease as my heart mellowed into a soft cushion of memories and peace. I had passed through yet another short space of time that was worthy of remembrance. Tucked away in my mind are all the past pictures of a life once lived as a couple. Accepting that past and all it held for me is an important part of my grief process. Memories return because we haven't forgotten our loved ones. Whenever we remember, I believe others seem to live again.

Every time we wish someone were with us, it bears witness to a relationship that was important to our well-being. Missing someone we've loved so much means we felt and cared deeply for them. While we sometimes wish the person was still with us in a more tangible way, would we really miss them so much if they were always by our side? Would we really have known then how much they meant to us? It was then, as my heart and mind returned to memories of the past, that I realized my husband was present in a different way. I didn't have to wish anymore. My wish had cone true.

Healing Moments

15

THE LAND OF OZ

I recently saw a wonderful stage production of The Wizard of Oz. I had always been a fan of the characters, especially Dorothy, who had an unusual zest for life and friendships. My late husband once said to me that I was the "Dorothy" in his life. Ruby shoes to take me anywhere along the yellow brick road and amazing new people to meet in the land of Oz were all I needed to keep me happy. I was even cast in a play once where my character dressed up in various Oz costumes as she cleaned house. My son-in-law reproduced a picture of an Oz album with my face as Dorothy, my husband as the scarecrow and my two daughters as the lion and the tin man. We had a lot of laughs over that picture, and it still sits on my mantel. Until my husband died, I hadn't realized how much I really felt like some of the characters from Oz during my grieving period.

After his death, I felt just like the scarecrow with no brain to figure out what direction I should take in life now that I was alone. I had a hard time processing simple things and felt confused much of the time. Although my heart was still intact, the tin man represented the broken heart that hurt for quite awhile. I knew I had a heart because I felt so many of the raw emotions that occur when someone you love so much leaves you behind. And who could forget the cowardly lion that represented the courage I had to find in order to face life alone without my best friend to help me along the way? I really felt fear loom over an already too sensitive heart, and now I had to find super strength to face new life issues.

As I watched Dorothy and her friends go down the yellow brick road looking for answers and a way to get home, I again related to finding a path where I could return to a more comfortable place. Little by little, as I walked the road of grief, I found my way to a more peaceful spot. By attending support groups and reading various books on bereavement, I became more clear and less confused in my thinking. By taking care of my personal needs, my broken heart began to mend. And finally, by following a path that wasn't always easy, I came to a point where I could see the world before me in a new light. I saw hope, possibilities and the love of new friends I've made along the way.

Healing Moments

16

WAVES OF GRIEF

Ocean waves are so strong at times, I fear what could happen if I were caught up in one of them. Standing on the shoreline, I've seen surfers challenge some of the largest waves off the coast of Hawaii, while I was intimidated by a much smaller wave in which probably I could have walked to shore in safety. Sometimes, being caught in a wave is not so threatening, but at other times one can be overwhelmed with fear. Once, I was actually caught up in one of those waves where the power of the water tossed me into a tumbling cycle that bruised and scratched my skin as I was thrown against the shell-crushed sand. Grateful to emerge intact, and covered with sand and seaweed, I felt embarrassed by my helplessness to get out of nature's watery grasp to safer ground as onlookers gasped.

Grief can be like those waves that tumble across the ocean. When my husband died, at first I felt like a tidal wave had grabbed hold of me as I was tossed back and forth from one strong emotional force to another. Just as I thought I'd recovered from the last hit, I was sent twirling again in a new bath of tears, unable to get grounded emotionally. At times, I felt I would drown in grief's grip. The fear that arose within kept me hostage for moments and even hours at times. It took time to break out of the hold uncertainty had on me. Obviously, my desire to live kept me struggling to get grounded. Somehow, I was going to get a foothold and survive this thrashing tidal wave. Little by little, as I inched my way to a more secure standing, I confidently embraced risks I had only dreamed about. I made up my mind to be an explorer in my new life as well as a researcher of the unknown. Each one of those new experiences taught me how to keep my head above the waves of grief that threatened to engulf and hold me hostage. I'm on drier land now, breathing better and struggling less to keep afloat.

Healing Moments

17

WHAT WILL I DO NOW?

During the time when my husband was dying, I reached out to others for help in coping with an unbearable situation. I felt lost in my struggle to find the right way to do some things. I lost confidence in my ability to navigate those right and left turns life seemed to give me periodically. After he died, I had recurrent thoughts of wondering what I would do now with my life? I had been on course with him most of my adult life. As a married couple, we arranged family, work and leisure time together. Now, I was left alone to sort out the "half" he had completed for me. What would I do now as I faced being alone trying to fill empty evenings? What would I do now if something in the house broke and I couldn't fix it? But mostly, what would I do with the rest of my life when all my future plans had revolved around us as a couple?

As I began the process of rebuilding my life, similar questions consumed much of my waking time. Often, I awoke in the middle of the night staring at the walls hoping they would provide the answers. Many times, I had to struggle through the feelings that surfaced when I was home alone and not busy. And many times I just couldn't control the pain of my loss, and I would have a crying time where the grief would flow in the form of tears. After a good cry, I usually felt better and managed to pull my thoughts together in a more positive mental framework.

As the days stretched into weeks and the weeks into months, I found myself solving problems, dealing more effectively with emotions, and growing more confident in my ability to handle life's losses. As long as I didn't rush into anything, an answer usually appeared at the right moment. I also found out that the question, "What will I do now?" can only be answered a day at a time and that's all I needed to focus on each day. After awhile, I came to appreciate the freedom to pick and choose, "What will I do now?" as I relaxed into a rhythm of my own making. Small accomplishments may have been the norm in the beginning of my grief journey, but now I have a full life and am wondering where the time goes.

Healing Moments

18

FAITH

The first time I walked into the bereavement group after my husband died, the room was full of strangers, and I looked around trying to see if there was someone I recognized. Only the coordinator of the group was familiar to me. I listened to each individual share the agony of their loss and when it was my turn to share, I felt a rush of emotions as I choked out the words. My body felt hot and my lack of composure began to betray me. I felt like running, so I quickly left the room thinking that my loss was too much to bear at the moment. Walking down the long hallway, I found another room to sit in for awhile and I composed myself. I didn't want anyone to see my grief or feel my pain as I had felt theirs. I also realized that if I didn't go back to the roomful of strangers, they couldn't become a roomful of friends.

The coordinator of the group allowed me time to process my deep emotions and then she encouraged me with her strength and love to return and face the others. Slowly, I put on my public face and gave myself permission to just listen for awhile as others spoke about their losses. As each person in the circle took time to share, I heard stories that reflected my own. I related to their pain and realized that shared loss helped me to know I wasn't the only grieving person around. There were many of us struggling with very similar issues. We were all bereaved and we chose to help each other by participating in a group process of healing from our sorrow. My faith began to increase again as I related to others.

As the weeks and months went by, I could feel the sorrow turn to laughter, excitement and joy, with new beginnings as well as funny experiences. What we once cried over had become a laughing matter in our "today" minds. New friendships were formed as we created a safe social atmosphere for our talks. We truly did receive as we gave each other comfort, support and hope. But most of all, our faith increased so that we could survive this passage into our new lives. Faith was the act of stepping into the unknown, which, in time, became the known. We all made faith our friend.

Healing Moments

19

MEMORIES

As I sat there at the restaurant counter, sipping a cup of warm coffee, I looked down the length of the side wall and noticed something hanging above the word "Banos" (or in English, bathroom). With sunken eyes, jagged, bared teeth, and huge horns, the dried cattle head looked exactly like the one I had at home. I remembered how excited my late husband had gotten when we walked by a Southwestern garden shop while on vacation. "That's really great, I've got to get one and have it shipped home," he said as he pointed at the cattle head with horns.

"You're joking!" I replied, knowing inside he was really serious. He had always liked the odd things that most others wouldn't buy, and this store had quite a supply of unusual artifacts.

The head hanging on the wall of the mission–style restaurant took me back in time for awhile. I remembered the trips we had taken to explore the Southwest territory. Fondness and gratitude filled my heart as I mentally revisited places my husband and I had enjoyed on our vacations: hiking, rock-climbing, exploring, lunches sitting next to a Joshua tree, and beautiful sunsets along the horizon as we meandered our way back to the cozy cottage we had rented for the night. Never needing to say a word, we felt united in the silence that drew us closer together as companions. It was truly a special experience for us, and when we returned home we both brought back mementos reminding us of our uniqueness.

Seeing that cattle head on the wall helped me to focus on the memories that encourage me to accept the times people share in relationships and what's really important in our daily lives. I'm grateful for having those times and appreciate them even more now as I look back. My daughter has the cattle head now because she also enjoys unique things, and I think it makes her feel closer to her dad. We each take what we need to remind us that our loved ones are still with us in our memories. I certainly have my fill of special times.

Healing Moments

20

LIFESAVERS

Evening rain had soaked the ground and as morning approached, I echoed back into the inquiring phone call, "I'm planning on leading the hike," It was my turn to lead the hiking group I had joined shortly after my husband had died. Getting out of the house and being with people was one of those lifesavers I embraced during those first months of intense grief. My late husband loved hiking and rock-climbing. We partnered up to expand our horizons and keep healthy. The group I joined had the same values, and I didn't want to hike alone.

After a couple of years of hanging out with others, I decided to lead my own hike. Familiar with many forested areas, I thought I had chosen a great spot. Still a novice though, I hadn't realized what an evening rain could do to a dry landscape that had been crunched under the feet of horses as well as tire tracks from bikes and wagons. Nonetheless, I had made the commitment, so I arrived with a plate of pastries to appease the early morning trekkers.

Three months earlier, I had imagined a crisp fall morning, vari-colored leaves and a panoramic view at the end of the hike where we could sit for awhile and admire the beauty. What I ended up with were three brave people who trudged through water-filled mud holes, wet pine branches brushing against faces and a steady, light rain. Even the forest animals were hiding out somewhere in a more comfortable environment.

By the end of the hike I was soaking wet, but I realized the three of us had made it through what life had actually given us that day, not what we had fantasized about. Had I not been the leader, I might not have gone on the hike and I would have missed the opportunity to learn more about the environment, about appropriate dress and about the fact that I could still go on in spite of the conditions. Trudging forth regardless of the "ups and downs" of life has given me strength, hope and courage to face difficult times without my partner. I've really learned to partner with myself.

Healing Moments

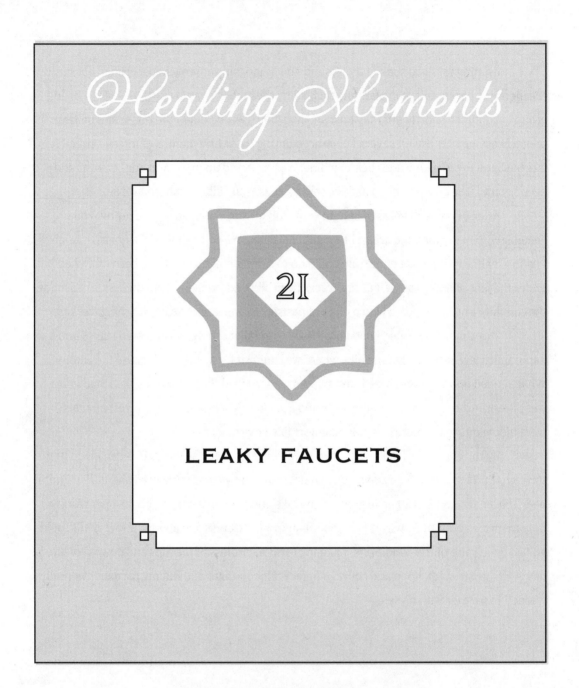

21

LEAKY FAUCETS

The yellow tape wrapped around the handles reminded me not to turn on the leaky bathroom faucet. I had started to fix the leak, but was unsuccessful at turning the too-tight joint below the sink. I had become the "handy woman" since my husband died. He was a "handyman" who was able to fix anything that broke. I really admired him, and I thought I could learn to do what he did. And, I did learn! Now, I know how to solder pipes, change electrical circuits, fix lawn mowers and broken windows, and the list goes on. After awhile, I felt like I could handle almost anything. The leaky sink and tub faucet had challenged me, though. "Another day," I thought. "Another day, I'll fix it; just not today."

Leaky faucets represent the petty annoyances that can get to you after awhile. It's just a small drip, but it's a reminder that something is broken or another problem needs attention. The trouble is as soon as you fix one problem, another arises too soon. Without my husband around, it felt like I was going under with all the problems to solve alone. The confidence and determination to singularly do it all began to affect me as I neglected the leaky sink and other areas. I just wouldn't give in to my own incompetence.

I just let the faucet drip, drip, drip until I finally asked a friend to fix it. Stronger than I was, he quickly pulled the joints apart as if he knew what he was doing and he had it glued it back together in a matter of a few hours. Months of anxiety and concern about the leaky sink washed down the drain as I paid the bill and humbled myself as a mediocre "handywoman." Actually, I felt relieved knowing I could hire this "handyman" any time I needed help with certain problems. I didn't really have to do it all myself. Trying to take care everything by myself was my way of feeling in control of a situation I really had no control over. I could learn to surrender to letting a "handyman" take care of what I couldn't do at the time. All I have to do is get tired of the drip, drip, drip.

Healing Moments

22

TRIGGERS

Old memories flooded my mind as I walked the concourse of the airport. It had been just a couple of years earlier that I had taken my first trip south for a needed break after my husband's death. Now, more than a year later, I walked the same concourse corridors with the same sights and sounds. Since this was my second flight alone, I had no old memories of traveling with my husband. I felt aglow as I found my way to the correct gate. After meandering a bit, I finally sat in one of the hard leather seats and relaxed while munching on an apple. From the overhead loudspeaker, I heard an attendant announce there was a gate change. Quickly, people began the trek to another gate quite a distance away. Nervously, I followed them up and down stairs and walkways until we arrived at a tram area that took us to our new departure gate. I wobbled as I climbed onto the tram.

The first memory of my late husband came when the woman next to me said she was from England. Telling her that my late husband and I had visited his family in the same city a few years earlier gave me a connection to my past. As we left the tram, I saw her again headed to the International section. Suddenly, suppressed feelings begin to surface as I walked past window displays of cultural artifacts. But, it wasn't until I reached the section heading toward a departure to Germany that I began to cry. My late husband was born in Germany, and I had always wanted to visit there with him. I looked up to see the city name of Stuttgart flashing behind the check-in counter. Instantly, reminders arose of tales that I had heard about the city and his family's life there. I actually looked around to see if I could find anyone who resembled him. I was looking for a human connection.

The grief I felt that day was nearly as intense as when he first died. Obviously, there are still some "triggers" that bring us back to earlier days. Maybe it was about some old memories; maybe, it was only about not having him to share new experiences with. Or just maybe, it was a way for me to know his presence is still here for me. All I know is that grief takes time, and moments like these are a part of the healing. Grief is a process of letting feelings surface long enough to deal with them and then going forward to another place of peace and calmness. That day, I relived some special moments, and I felt less sorrow.

23

BUSY, BUSY

For months after my husband died, I kept myself very busy with work, projects and new undertakings, thinking all along that I was moving on with my new life. I was moving, but not mourning. I kept myself so busy that I lost touch with some important aspects of my "self." My "self" had a value system. My "self" had a belief system. And my "self" was lost from all the running. When death happens, we often keep ourselves busy thinking that busyness is our source of strength and comfort. What we really need to do is be still for awhile. We need to be in touch with our feelings about the death and how death affects us now. We need to be still in order to make an assessment.

When I finally became still, the feelings began to emerge from deep within the center of my being. At first I was scared, believing I'd never overcome the hurt I felt. I was angry because I was in this situation without a companion to help me. Also, I felt guilty that maybe I hadn't done enough to help him in his last days. The more still I was, the more feelings emerged, and I felt awful for a long time. But, slowly I began to feel better and gradually I regained my "self." I really had to examine who I was before I could own my new identity. Moving on doesn't necessarily mean a new career, a new job or a new home environment. Moving on is a personal growth experience that might encompass physical changes. For me, it means knowing who I was before and who I am after losses. Moving on is integrating the change death brings into our lives, as well as adjusting to the everyday ups and downs of life as we face our new beginnings.

Healing Moments

24

DEEPLY ROOTED

Snow and ice had fallen from the rooftop, crushing the small, barren tree on the side of my house. I thought about how I might be able to rescue it if only I could chop away at the mound of icy snow. But I couldn't even get to the area because of another pile of snow covered stairs leading to the tree. I felt immobilized as I sat there in my car studying the tender branches that were already showing signs of budding for spring. Probably the tree would survive the crushing blows of winter's fury because it was deeply rooted, but it caused me to ponder surviving the hardship death causes us at times.

Other family deaths that had occurred in the past few years and I had survived the impact of grief, but sometimes I felt crushed and overwhelmed by the weight of grief's blanket. I thought I'd never come out of the shock or denial that covered me like the sheet of ice on that small tender tree. As I looked at that tree again, I thought about the beating it had taken and I thought about its root system going deep into the earth, holding its life force together where it was warmer. I also had deep roots that would carry my life force into the warmth of my future. I had the stamina, perseverance and character that had been forged from other death experiences. I learned to be patient with the grief process as well as tolerant of life's mysteries. I could make it again.

Glancing once more at the small tree, I knew it would survive, and that gave me the hope I needed to live this one day as fully and joyfully as I possibly could. My life force is connected to nature just as it is for that tree that was once a seedling. I too can have the confidence that my roots go deep into emotional, intellectual, physical and spiritual soil that will sustain me in the winters of my grief. I will hold on to life and appreciate the ability to regenerate through nature's life force.

Healing Moments

25

HOLIDAYS

While walking through the aisles of the grocery store, a display of Halloween costumes caught my attention. Halloween usually kicks off the holiday season, but it still felt like summer, and I wasn't ready to face another holiday without my spouse. Halloween had been one of his favorite times. He loved watching the little children dress up in their favorite costumes, and he loved eating the treats that we handed out. At times, he was very generous and gave two or three pieces to each child, but when the container became less filled, he worried about not having enough and disappointing the next child. Watching him run to the door like a child himself, I delighted in his expression of joy and his comments about the children's costumes.

The first few years after he died, I hadn't wanted to continue the tradition. I would make sure the lights were off in the house as I left for the evening, hoping to discourage the mask-covered children. When I arrived home later, I said, "Another year of that gone."

When Thanksgiving came, I made reservation at a restaurant out of town. "At least I would be able to get out of cooking," I decided, but I felt a little guilty. I reasoned that I would avoid all those fattening leftovers that we both had enjoyed for days after, and there would be no mess to clean up. It made me feel good to go out for the day. Before he died, my husband and I usually hosted family gatherings that lasted way into the evening. Now, my "family" included strangers sitting side by side at sterile tables where we could get up as often as we liked and go to a buffet line filled with delectable delights. With my mind focused on the food, I didn't have to think about those who were not present.

As one holiday came to a close and another loomed on the horizon, I adjusted to a new normal that changed the family dynamics. At first the loneliness and awkwardness seemed too uncomfortable to face and I wanted to run away. "But how long can I run from the grief?" I asked myself. I knew I had to face the awkwardness and the pain of another changed holiday. And I have to face the fact that my circumstance includes a loved one who is no longer there to share in any tangible way. Facing that reality was the best thing I could do for myself and for those whom I loved and who loved me. In time, my spirit was lifted again as I engaged in making new holiday memories with renewed strength and hope.

26

STOLEN MOMENTS

The couple sat there at the small, cozy table eating and talking. They seemed more intense when certain topics were discussed. For the most part though, they appeared to be happy being together for those few moments of their day. Holding hands, smiling, and gazing deeply into each other's eyes, I sensed a special kind of love between them.

I drifted back in time to familiar setting where my late husband and I would meet in the middle of the day to connect with each other in that same special way. Even after thirty-four years of a relationship, we still looked forward to those refreshing moments we shared that ignited the fiery glow of love. We drew strength from each other as we planned trips and discussed children, family or work issues. But, most of all, it was knowing that this was a very special marital relationship that bonded our memories for life. In the giving and taking, we created something unique and everlasting, even unto death.

That was a special time in our lives, and since his death I have realized how special those moments were in the lasting memories of our marriage. "Stolen moments" made me feel that I had been graced with love. "Stolen moments" helped me to get through some of those tough days when I saw other couples walking hand-in-hand as we had, too. And "stolen moments" provided the strength I needed to be alone in a world of so many who want what I had. I feel lucky to have loved and been loved with stolen moments.

I still get teary-eyed when I think about those times as I continue to grieve his death and the loss of someone so precious. It was wonderful to have had such an intimate connection. When I see others who are embraced by "stolen moments" I feel happy for them, because I know the meaning of their everlasting love. The sincere gift of that kind of love lasts forever in our hearts.

Healing Moments

27

Echoes

My late husband and I used to go hiking in the western part of the United States where canyon lands stretch for miles across rugged, colorful terrain. It was fun to come around a bend in the road and find a cave where petroglyphs were etched in the rocks. As we climbed into the area, deep ravines would loom before us, and we were awed by what we saw. Inevitably, one of us would let out a scream and the sound would bounce off rock-wall formations and ring back in echo form. We'd continue for a long time feeling extremely powerful that our voices could carry so far. Occasionally, we'd let out a huge laugh at our childish antics.

Since he died, I haven't had the time or opportunity to go back out west and explore those areas again. Nonetheless, I can still hear the echoes of his voice when he'd come home from work at the end of the day and call my name. I can still hear the echoes of memories where we shared just sitting together on a couch reading a book or watching television. When I look out at my backyard, I can still hear the echoes of a man mowing a lawn, digging a hole for a tree and building a picturesque garden designed by loving hands where flowers bloom from spring till late fall. In fact, his echoes surround me when I turn my thoughts toward him and the memories we made of a life lived together while raising a family. The sound of those echoes are still dear to me even after I've regained a new sense of myself, separate from the experiences we used to enjoy together.

The echoes of my past are fulfilling and I can look back fondly on those times. I still hike, but with a new group of people who enjoy the outdoors. And I have found that we all have stories of echoes in some form that gently nudge us to remember the good times.

Healing Moments

28

HOLDING ON

I recently read an expression about grief from another author that made me laugh with amusement. I thought, "It's true, we all stay in our own "house of grief." I don't really grieve like others do, that's for sure! I'm an emotional, private person who often puts up my guard in public places. I have also had a different relationship with the deceased, whether it is a family member or friend. But, most of all, my grief is about who I am as an individual. When it comes to the expression of my grief, who I am has to do with how much or how often I want to show my suffering face to the world. Who I am is not how I babble about being a grieving widow, sibling, daughter or grandparent. Who I am is about how I'm "holding on" as I pass through a process of life-changing events, especially when death occurs.

"Holding on" may seem to be a foreign term to equate with grief, yet isn't that what I do when I run around keeping busy? If I don't, I may go under, never to rise again in order to meet life on life's terms. For me, "holding on" is a way to keep me occupied until some time passes so I can absorb the "nightmare of thoughts" that swirl in my head. Or, maybe "holding on" gives me needed rest from the trauma associated with wondering how I am truly going to handle this "hole" in my heart that is so big I'll never get it mended. There's an empty spot where those I've interacted with are gone; all I have left are their memories. Those memories help fill the empty spot like a vase filled with a bouquet of flowers, plus a wonderful fragrance. That's worth a whole lot of "holding on"!

So, what do I hold onto? I hold on to memories of their smiles, laughter, excitement and interactions as if they were here with me as I walk alone. The pictures on the mantel, phone recordings, videos and albums help me to hold on as I work through my grief and come to some sort of reconciliation about their passing. Holding on supports me and encourages me to reach out to others who know the emptiness of grief and who share a common bond of what holding on means to them. That's my "house of grief." I live there in that house and "holding on" helps.

Healing Moments

29

TIME PIECES

I was in a clock repair shop recently where there were hundreds of various styles of time pieces hanging on walls or sitting on counter tops, ready for pick-up. As I looked at the huge display, I wondered about why no one had come to retrieve the pieces. They surely couldn't have belonged to the shop owner. There were just too many!

The variety of shapes and sizes was amazing. Each timepiece carried a unique signature of the maker and each had an unusual design, and each had the currently appropriate time. Each was in perfect working order, ticking, chiming and spinning in synchronicity. I felt good among the harmony of such inanimate objects as though they spoke of some mysterious moment when they fell silent, unable to generate motion or sound. Now, they were all in working order in a cacophony of sound.

I thought about whenever I've experienced the death of someone precious in my life; the internal timepiece in my heart stopped ticking for a while. We were really the same, this clock and my heart, as we sought repair from a master technician. In the case of the timepieces, a spare part might restore it to full repair, but when it comes to a broken heart, only time can restore it to a new working order. The time it takes depends upon me and the depth and breadth of the relationship I had with the deceased.

The memories, the death circumstances, the support systems, and time are all part of that depth and breadth of the repair process. Like the clock, the new parts affect the working order and are precisely made for each clock. Since I am unique in my healing from grief, I need special repair from the Master Technician of time. Healing will take place as I honor my grief process. I honor my grief by acknowledging feelings, relationships, life and new beginnings and endings. Time will heal the wounds of my broken heart. Each aspect of my personality is precisely tuned for healing at the right time. I will give myself much time, and time will heal the wounds. I can trust that, like the clocks and watches in the repair shop, I too will get back to working order.

Healing Moments

30

Isolation

There are periods in my grief journey where I need to isolate for a while. I need to go home, away from the crowds of working, partying and scurrying people who do not have a clue as to what is going on with me. In fact, I'm not even sure what's going on with me sometimes as I get caught up in the energy swirl of life. Whether it's the people, the climate of happiness and tension others exude or the particular event. Sometimes, I just need to go home and release whatever I've absorbed before I can present my face to the world again.

In that isolation, I can go to a quiet place where I might reflect upon the memories of those who are now gone. In isolation, I can allow myself feelings I may need to express privately. Maybe, in that isolation, I can pretend that my world is really fine, that nothing has changed and that those I've loved have not died—just like a child might do. I can focus on what might work to help myself. Isolation doesn't necessarily mean I'm sick with grief and it has taken over my life, as others might think. Isolation can truly be a place of recovery where I can be restored to a better place, emotionally as well as physically.

At times, isolation may appear as if I've gone into a closet in order not to face the reality of what has happened, but I need that closet for awhile to protect me from the icy cold, blistery winds of grief that threaten my recovery from the loss of those I've loved. Without the coziness that isolation provides, the shock of grief could destroy my inner security. Isolation helps to protect my inner self, providing me with renewed strength to make meaning out of my new world. As I get more comfortable with my new surroundings, as I adapt, adjust and change, I'll be out again.

Healing Moments

31

SMALLER CIRCLES

The spring's warmth had begun to melt the snow accumulated in my back yard. One day, after a wet snowstorm had left an abundance of the white stuff, I made a large snowman just for fun. I thought it would help me to measure time. How long would it take to melt? How long would that large round circle grow smaller and smaller until there was nothing left? Where did the melting ice go as this inanimate object decreased? These were the thoughts swirling around in my mind. Then, my mind began to grasp the significance of the melting snowman. Death had decreased the circle of family and friends over the years, and I pondered the thought for awhile.

My family had once been a large circle of siblings, parents, spouses, cousins and a grandchild. Now, the family circle had decreased as death stole some of them, changing the energy force for those left behind. Empty spots around the dining room table marked the family gatherings, especially noticeable during special occasions. Laughter and small talk also had decreased where loud energy had once filled the air. Part of me longed for the old times again, but I knew that those times were gone. Now, only phantom memories of an earlier period existed. Now, all that existed were smaller circles.

As I thought about the smaller circles, the snowman came to mind again. Once larger, it had decreased into a small puddle of new energy that would provide sustenance to the grass roots below ground. Even though, visibly, the snowman was gone, the thought renewed my energy and I felt connected. Maybe all I really needed was to remember the larger circles of friends and family, as well as all the good times we had. Just like that snowman, the circles are still there in special ways. All I need to do is remember the larger circles for a connection. I will remember!

Healing Moments

32

MENTAL SHIFTS

I had been talking to an old friend of mine who had moved away shortly after the death of my spouse. I remember how terrible I felt at the time because of losing her, too. As we continued the conversation she commented on how good I sounded. "You sound so good, you sound so good," she kept saying. For the first time in a long time, I could honestly respond back positively, believing that I was good. It was then that I told her I had had another mental shift and was seeing the world in a new way. "Sometimes, especially when we're going through grief, we see through a broken lens, don't we, she responded.

I thought about the concept of a broken lens, but I related more to a dusty, dirty window. It seemed for long time everything I came into contact with had the covering of that same grimy film. That image became very clear as I remembered just a few hours earlier I had been at an exercise class in the basement of a church where I was paying more attention to a dirty window. As I watched people pass by, I could only see vague images. Then, I realized that grief is like a dirty window. A mental shift had taken place at some point where I couldn't see clearly. I truly had my own mental, dirty window of images.

I knew that the people I work, live and play with were like those strangers walking by that grimy basement window. Somehow, I had lost an intimate connection and couldn't let them into my thoughts or feelings. That mental shift had somehow clouded my window, even though I knew they wanted to help me through my struggles. I guess when I finally worked through some of the painful aspects of grief privately, as so many of us do, I was able to have another mental shift where the window of my mind was washed with the tears of grief. When my friend made the comment, "you sound so good," I knew I had come to a better place in my life. Since I now have an improved understanding and acceptance of death, my mind's window has fewer spots. I have a much clearer focus. I feel good, I sound good, and I am good. And I'm connecting with people, places and life again with a cleaner window due to my "mental shift."

Healing Moments

33

THE SHOW MUST GO ON

There's a saying in the theatrical world that "the show must go on." I learned that phrase when I took an acting class in college. In spite of what happens in the day-to-day life of an actor, he or she must create another reality while on stage in order to keep the performance going. There were a few times I wanted to stop the show I was in due to untimely circumstances in my real world. Too often, life seems to give us experiences where we are forced to show up in spite of our natural inclination to bail out.

The painful experience of death is one of those times when the real world calls us forward as we put up a brave front for others. When my husband died, I did not want to stand in line to receive "well-wishers" nor did I want to lead the processional as the family walked into the church for the memorial service. And, I certainly did not want to face the weeks after the funeral was over and people had gone on to their normal lives while I was left to figure out a new role for myself. I had just lost the most important roles of my life as wife, lover, confidant, friend, caretaker, etc. What new role would I play now, except the grieving widow and for who knows how long?

These are the times where I see "the show must go on" and I'm triggered into a reality I don't want. The roles we play in our day-to-day existence are often the hardest. These are the real performances where we have to act as if our lives are fine in spite of what we truly feel inside. After all, the world doesn't stop turning because of our grief. So, after awhile, we really do need to move on with our lives, adjusting to the new roles we play as creatively as possible. Imagination gives our inner self the strength to create new experiences that will help us on our grief journey. The world is our stage. We can create a happier ending. The world is watching and will applaud our efforts.

About the Author

Mary Nowyj has a Master's degree in communication skills from Syracuse University in her hometown. She has worked in academia teaching and tutoring both American and international students. An active volunteer in her community, she has given her time and talents in various ways to theater, literacy programs, public broadcasting and environmental issues. Hope For The Bereaved, a grief support organization based in Syracuse, New York, is one of her favorites because of their compassion and concern for others as a "grief support help line." Mary loves to travel and is always looking for a new adventure for personal growth.

www.centering.org
www.i-remember.org